INDONESIA

FROM THE AIR

Typeset by Superskill, Singapore
Printed in Singapore by Tien Wah Press
Colour Separation by Columbia Offset

ISBN: 9971-40-028-6
Inquiries should be directed to:
TIMES EDITIONS (S) PTE LTD
422 Thomson Road, Singapore 1129, Tlx: EDTIME RS 37908,
Tel: 2550011

or

PT HUMPUSS DIVISI PERIKLANAN HANURATA GRAHA,
Ground Floor, Jalan Kebon Sirih, 67-69 Jakarta 10340, Indonesia.
Tel: 327490-327042 Tlx: HAV. IA 45273

INDONESIA
FROM THE AIR

INTRODUCTION BY ACHMAD TAHIR

TEXT BY ARSWENDO ATMOWILOTO

PHOTOGRAPHED BY DIANE GRAHAM GARTH,
LEONARD LUERAS, KAL MULLER, LUCA INVERNIZZI TETTONI,
DICKY WP, ALAIN COMPOST AND EMMO ITALIAANDER

EDITED BY DANA LAM

DESIGNED BY LEONARD LUERAS

PUBLISHED BY PT HUMPUSS AND TIMES EDITIONS
FIRST EDITION 1986

This is what Samosir Island, Lake Toba and the surrounding North Sumatra countryside south of the city of Medan look like to aerial survey photographers from an altitude of 800 kilometers, or 25,000 feet. The "false color" photo was taken in June, 1982 by the Landsat MSS. The scale of the picture, which is used for cartographic purposes, is 1:50,000. Legend: Red: Forests and plantations; Dark Blue: Water; Light Blue: Paddy fields and other cultivations; Green: Rock and bare land; Pink: Grasslands, bush and kampungs.

Contents

INTRODUCTION

The country of Indonesia is best known for its fabled island, Bali, yet few are aware that Bali is but one of 13,677 islands that comprise Indonesia. Many may remember reading of the massive eruption of Krakatau in 1883, or of prehistoric dragons still alive on Komodo, but again, they probably do not realize that these are still only two of the many thousands of islands in the Indonesian Archipelago. Likewise, every schoolchild learns of the Spice Islands, and readers of adventure books know of the wild jungles of Borneo, but if you ask them where these islands are, they will probably say, vaguely, "Somewhere in the East".

Indonesia needs books of introduction like *Indonesia From The Air* to show the world that these exotic, disparate islands are part of one vast nation. But most books trying to show the entire archipelago too often confuse the reader. The nation is too vast, too diversified, multicolored and multi-faceted to be swallowed in one gulp. Indonesia's terrain ranges from tropical jungles to snow-covered peaks, and the cultures, customs and languages of her people may differ every 100 kilometers.

Too often, a book trying to compress all of these elements into a few hundred pages cannot show Indonesia as a nation with one identity. Reading such a book is like looking out the window of an express train. One fascinating image is too quickly replaced by another, flashing by with such speed that the reader cannot understand how these vistas fit together.

Indonesia From the Air is different. From the air, we can see the big picture. By looking down on the islands from the skies, we see similarities which are often not apparent from ground level. Rice fields are much the same throughout the archipelago, as is the farmer's relationship to the land. From the Strait of Malacca to the Banda Sea, fishermen — whether Javanese, Bugis or Florenese — are all "Champions of the Sea".

Indonesians say: "We are many, but we are one", which is also our national motto: "Unity in Diversity". From the air you can see this unity, and how so many different people have formed one nation.

As an introduction to Indonesia, this book is appropriate in another sense. For most visitors, their first view of Indonesia is from the air. Ninety-five percent of all foreign arrivals are through the airports of Jakarta, Medan and Bali. Therefore, it is important that Indonesia be beautiful from the air because an increasing number of visitors come not only to buy our products, or participate in our national development, but for another purpose — tourism.

Situated on one of the great marine crossroads of the world — between Europe, China and the Pacific — foreigners have come in large numbers to Indonesia throughout history. Indonesians have a great sense of hospitality; we open our arms to guests while keeping firmly to our customs and beliefs. Though modern tourists may sometimes seem to invade a destination, Indonesians regard them with welcome as corps of engineers building bridges of understanding.

The very nature of the tourism industry is based on cooperation and mutual understanding. As tourism affects so many areas of the nation and the government — communications, immigration, manpower, conservation — a close working relationship is needed between government agencies and both domestic and foreign sectors.

In keeping with this spirit of cooperation, many government departments and commercial establishments have participated in the production of this beautiful, sensitive portrait of the Indonesian archipelago from the air. It is our hope that this book will now inspire its readers to experience the beauty of Indonesia for themselves.

— Achmad Tahir
Minister of Tourism, Post and Telecommunications
Republic of Indonesia.

Top Left: A formation of early Dutch military aircraft fly over sawah, ricefields, in Central Java. Bottom Left: a KNILM aircraft flying over Mount Lamongan in East Java. KNILM, a subsidiary of KLM, established commercial aviation in Indonesia in 1928.

Top Right: Hutama MP Soeharto cruises through Indonesian air space in a recreational Ultra-Light aircraft. Bottom Right: A modern airplane built by Indonesia's own IPTN Nusantara aviation firm. Far Right: An Indonesian-built Gatari helicopter hovers over rice-fields around Jakarta.

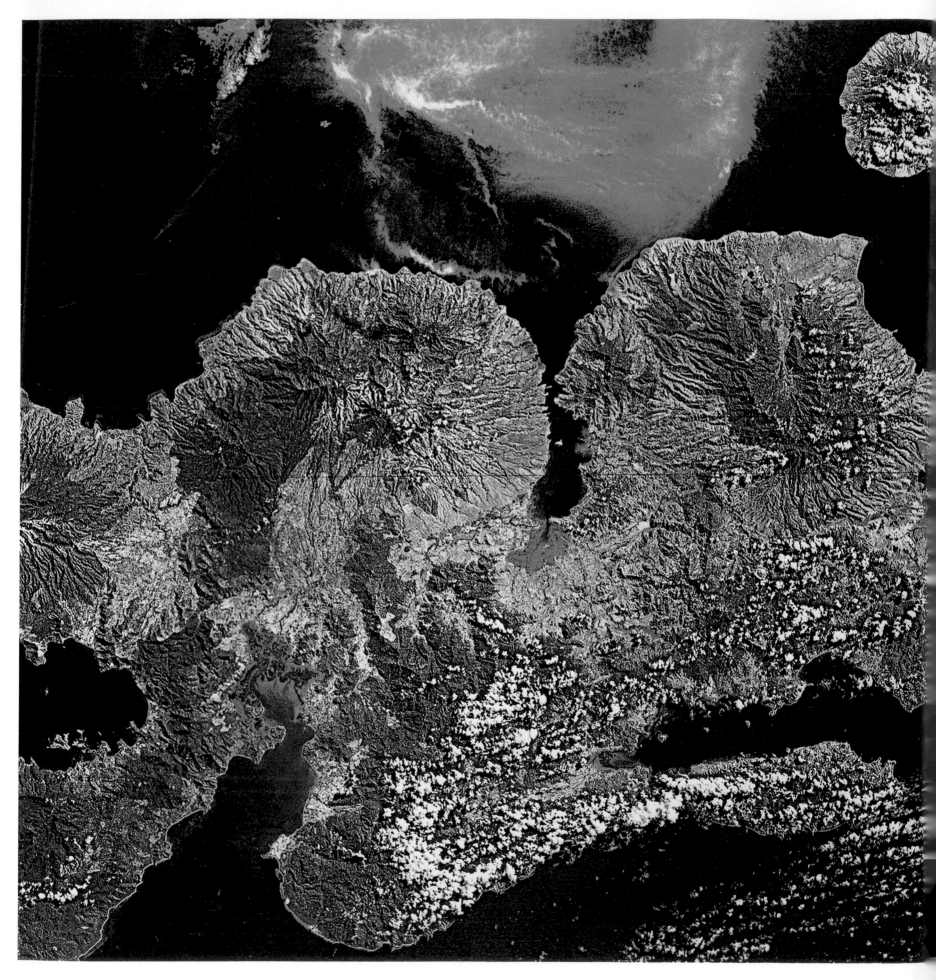

12

Left: A satellite view of parts of Nusa Tenggara. The big landmass to the left is eastern Sumbawa. Komodo, abode of the earth's last "dragons" is the irregularly shaped island to the right. A close-up of this most inhospitable island appears overleaf. A small fraction of western Flores is to the extreme right of this "false-color" photograph taken from an altitude of 800 kilometers or 25,000 feet in June 1982 by Landsat MSS.

A VIEW FROM ABOVE

INDONESIA FROM THE AIR. Why not? Only from the dizzying heights of a bird in flight can we appreciate the immense scale of this colorful nation: 13,677 islands strung over 5,760 kilometers of tropical sea and offering a spectrum of cultures and landscapes rarely paralleled in the world. The archipelago was once upon a time known to explorers and bounty-hunters as The Spice Islands. The very name echoed promises of fame and fortune and early visitors to these islands included such illustrious persons as Fa Hsien (414 AD), Marco Polo (1292), Ferdinand Magellan (1600) and Captain James Cook (1770).

Today, to see Indonesia, we can choose to fly Garuda, the country's national airline (named after the mythical eagle-symbol of Indonesia) or take-off on the magical wings of the legendary Gatotkaca. Who is Gatotkaca? He is a celebrated hero, an oft-applauded figure in Indonesian folklore and a resounding star in *wayang kulit* — shadow puppet theatre — the oldest of the art forms that make up Indonesia's unmistakable and enchanting character.

In modern terms, Gatot — with affection — is a kind of all-seeing native superman. Legend has it that he wanders about the "seven levels of heaven" constantly, keeping perpetual watch over his beloved country. He is idolized by all. Indeed, a giant statue of Gatot, erected by Indonesia's first President, Soekarno, still stands at a major intersection in Jakarta and an Indonesian-made aircraft has been christened Tutuka, Gatot's childhood nickname.

To fly with Garuda would, admittedly, be a quick way out. But to fly with Gatotkaca, on a private tour of his multi-textured Indonesia, would constitute an extraordinary adventure.

At 20,000 feet above sea-level, all you will see of Indonesia is blue and green — great expanses of blue sea and forested mountains luxuriating in the equatorial sun. Upon closer look, other colors emerge in a coy, infinite interplay of shades and tones. Azure. Ultramarine. Lime.

Emerald. Indonesia is just so, a much-the-same surface enveloping wide variations on a theme, a vast complexity with an underlying unity.

Blue. The Indonesian Archipelago lies between the world's two biggest oceans — the Pacific Ocean and the Indian Ocean. To the north, the light blue Java sea laps at thick mangrove swamps; to the south, deep blue breakers rise to crash — white — against cliffsides and dazzling sands. Small wooden houses line these beaches like so many matchbox-structures of a child's play. But these are real houses, housing real families.

From their doors and from their windows, wives and children wait for and call out to *bapak* as he returns home. It's a domestic story that never changes. The fisherman-father returning from his day at sea is almost certainly the grandchild of an older seaman, a maritime descendant of the old Majapahit and Sriwijayan Empires, the founding fathers of old Indonesia.

Green. Dense, sweltering primary forests dominate Sumatra, Kalimantan, Sulawesi and Irian Jaya. Watered by two generous monsoons (a northeast monsoon which blows from November to April and a southeast monsoon from May to October), these rainforests blanket 65 percent of Indonesia's total land area of two million square kilometers. Looking on from the air, the dark green of vast forest canopies stretches from horizon to horizon symbolically preserving the enigmatic, eclectic world below.

Green is a restful color, equally welcomed by the fatigued airborne visitor and the analytical and earthbound economist. In Indonesia, it is a color that represents a trusted source of riches. A large proportion of Indonesia's exports comes from the forests. Teak and other hardwoods which make up this very canopy now seen from the air might be felled tomorrow and sold in a variety of forms. Indonesia is the world's largest producer and exporter of plywood and timber has, for a very long time, been an important income earner along side rubber, copra, bauxite, palm oil and petroleum. But, overzealous logging has taken its toll.

17

Soil erosion is a serious problem and, in response, the Indonesian government is encouraging selective cutting and reforestation. Six percent of the nation's land has been set aside as nature reserve and national parks.

At the edge of the forest, tapestries of blue-green ricefields sparkle in the early morning light. A farmer stands in his field, in knee-deep water that carries nutrients to his soil and guarantees his survival. He is content, for his rice flourishes and grows like a dream.

From Java to Bali, ricefields — or *sawah* — are sectioned into rectangles of differing sizes. Low dikes and earthmounds give the plains a living texture, as though the gods have created a cubistic masterpiece from the earth. This is, however, not merely Art for Art's sake. Underlying the aesthetics is a subsistence culture that has changed Indonesia from a rice-importing country to a self-sufficient country capable of feeding its millions of citizens.

In Bali, an ancient and complex irrigation method called *subak* ensures that each farmer receives sufficient water for his crops. You cannot see this, but you can sense it in collective smiles, even as the Balinese continue to toil with tools old enough for a permanent place in foreign museums.

In East Java and Nusa Tenggara, savannah lands counterpoint the lushness of Java proper and Bali. Along the coasts of southern Sumatra and Kalimantan, wetlands, once dismissed as worthless swamp, now play a wide-ranging and recognized ecological role. Throughout the archipelago, mountain ranges tower and loom above all, and volcanoes, like so many paradoxes in Indonesia, spew life and death.

When you are a part of the Pacific Ocean's "Ring of Fire," tragedy and blessings regularly befall you hand-in-hand. Indonesia has more volcanoes than any country in the world. The imposing Merapi breathes ominously over Yogyakarta, monitored by four vulcanology stations. On the other hand, Tangkubanperahu is a commercially viable tourist attraction, and Krakatau — having burnt itself out in one of

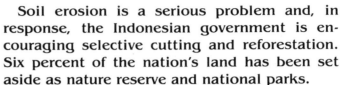

Left: The Bengawan Solo, longest river in Java, celebrated in history and song, meanders through lush ricefields in the heart of Central Java. For centuries Java's primary waterway, the Bengawan Solo's stately flow and complex turnings mirror the character of the Javanese, who value refinement, indirectness, and an unhurried pace.

19

Right: 'Champions of the Sea'. Indonesians are married to the sea – the Sultan of Yogyakarta traditionally trysts with Loro Kidul, Queen of The Southern Sea, to reconfirm the relationship between his people and the mighty Indian Ocean.

history's most devastating explosions — has risen, literally from the ashes as the younger Anak Krakatau, a natural laboratory unrivaled in the world. Mount Bromo, meanwhile, is a pilgrimage point for the Tenggerese, the direct descendants of the great Hindu Empires.

Every few years a volcano erupts to wreak devastation on some unsuspecting area and refugees stream down escape roads or take to the sea in resignation, leaving behind houses, farms and sometimes loved ones buried in the lava. But the refugees return soon enough, for they know that it is the volcanic ash that gives Indonesian soil its fertility. The monsoon rains flush everything into the sea, and without the periodic outpourings of the volcanoes, all Java and Bali would be left barren.

In the shadow of volcanoes, at the edge of ricefields, and encroaching on wetlands and coastlines, towns and cities grow and continue to grow at an unprecedented speed. Jakarta, Surabaya, Medan, Balikpapan, Ujung Pandang — all are interchangeable with alien expanses of red-tiled roofs in the surrounding green.

Each day, an endless stream of buses carry villagers to their new life in the cities. Like moths to a flame, they desert their peaceful villages for the bright city lights. But unlike moths, who immolate themselves when they reach their goal, the newcomers smile at whatever small improvement the city gives their lives. How can they smile without a steady job; with hungry wives and hungry children? Perhaps they cannot conceive of unhappiness, for in Indonesian, the expression for "to frown" is the same as "to smile".

From the air, the city is not dissimilar to the village. In the village, streams meander around clusters of houses; in the city, roads cut through neighborhoods. Rivers flow alongside villages, connecting them to the outside; expressways encircle the cities. Both are dangerous. In the village, crossing a river, you could be eaten by a crocodile; in the city, crossing a road, you might be run over by a bus. Traffic victims regularly add up to record numbers. Be careful when you

cross the road in Jakarta. Red lights can mean simply "to go faster", and a left turn signal could mean the driver is about to do any of several things: turn right, go straight or make a U-turn. Ironically, traffic safety is taught from grade school; but the road is not a schoolroom.

SUMATRA FROM THE AIR. Starting from Aceh, the northernmost tip of the Indonesian archipelago, the first sign of human habitation on this vast island (third largest in Indonesia and fifth largest in the world) are Gayo houses. These houses are built on sixteen pillars and their doors always point north, in the direction of Mecca. Aceh is the most heavily Islamic part of Indonesia. There is a Mosque and dormitory in every built-up area and the saying is: "If you can't get to Mecca, going to Aceh is the next best thing."

To the south of Aceh is Batak land. Batak houses are often huge in order to house the traditionally enormous and continually extending Batak families. They are also divided into two sides. One side, for the womenfolk, is entered by the front. The men's side, meanwhile, is entered from beneath.

Bataks are renowned for their lung-power, an asset they put to good use in calling out to each other from their houses. In the city, the Batak's powerful voice is heard shouting out destination points above the din of bus passengers. Bataks mostly work as bus conductors in Jakarta, and though their vehicles run on fixed routes with route numbers and destination points prominently displayed in front, the enthusiastic Batak-conductors still feel obliged to give passengers verbal reminders. Just as well, too. The labour force of 65 million people increases by 2.8 percent every year. If passengers did not want to be shouted at, there would be higher unemployment all round. As it is, the Batak's clannish tradition acts as a kind of buffer on the unemployment rate. One Batak is always welcome in the house of another and looked after till he finds independent means. So, when one Batak owns a bus, he can have as many as three conductors — all at the same time.

Away from Batak territory, in the highlands of West Sumatra, another type of house is readily distinguishable from the air. Sagging in the middle with horns at either end, the roof of the Minangkabau's *rumah gadang* looks much like the top of a buffalo's head.

The Minangs are matrilineal folk. Women both own and rule the house. Husbands merely live there. Bachelors, by the way, sleep in mosques. Most Minang men, however, have begun the long road to liberation. Away from their home villages, they mostly turn up as successful owners of Padang restaurants, selling the delectable cuisine that is Indonesia's most famous. Spicy Padang food is also Indonesia's most ubiquitous. Indonesians like to say that when Neil Armstrong took that famous first step onto the moon, there was already a Padang restaurant there.

There were probably also *kaki lima,* — hawker carts — another business popular with Minang men. A Minang starting his itinerant business will have his goods spread out on a sheet of newspaper at the roadside. Five years later nothing will have changed. This does not mean he is unsuccessful. Rather, it is merely a question of priorities. A Minang man seldom uses profits to expand his business. Instead, he sends any earnings beyond a basic living wage back to his village. As a result, many a *gadang* house now basks beneath zinc or asbestos roofings — proud symbols of their owners' success — even though palm leaves provided cooler shelter in the past. In Minang country, a zinc roof is a status symbol.

Continuing southeast, the highlands descend into the steamy, muddy lowlands of South Sumatra. Flat and featureless except where a wide, tea-color river snakes its nonchalant way through the jungle, this is oil country and Sumatra's richest and most primitive part. Most of South Sumatra is wild, isolated and, outside of the towns, lawless.

Palembang, on the River Musi, is the metropolis and Indonesia's richest city. If we took a dive with our guide Gatot, some of the city's riches

Left: Anak Krakatau. The Son of Krakatau emerged from the sea 50 years after the original island blew itself to pieces in 1883. It is now a matchless natural laboratory where scientists study how life takes hold on virgin land.

27

might be distinguishable. A US$200 million petrochemical complex rises from the landscape of Plaju, while a massive refinery at Sungei Gerong turns out no less than 275,000 barrels of crude oil a day. There is also a television station, a sports stadium, a clock tower and the elegant minaret of the city's main mosque to make a citizen proud.

Other settlements of about 5,000 strong hug the river for dear life, for it is the river that gives them sustenance. Apart from precious, multipurpose water, the river brings to town — twice a week — the excitement of the floating supermarkets. These come in the form of two barges lashed on either sides of a tugboat and filled to the brim with produce from neighboring farms. Business is, understandably, brisk.

From other aerial vantages, new "rivers" are visible, pushing their aggressive, garrulous way through the jungle. A journey that took a day by boat now takes an hour by bus on new jungle roads. The Trans-Sumatran Highway, for example, is bringing the 21st century to 19th century South Sumatra, seemingly dislocating all in its path. As a result, for the first time in their lives, natives of groups such as the Kubu tribe are coming into the open, forced by the inexorable forces of these asphalt "rivers" to leave the protective confines of their familiar jungle.

JAVA FROM THE AIR. In one fell swoop, a delighted Gatot will point to the vast attractions of this 132,187 square kilometer island with few reservations. Java is renowned for its exotic cultures, its arts, its dances, its history, and its lush, tropical beauty. In the hills, sprawling rainforests give way to alpine meadows, and in the lowlands, padi fields and tobacco plantations converge with fragrant spice fields in an endless montage of nature at her artistic best. On the skyline, volcanoes loom grey and majestic, and at places such as Parangtritis, black sand dunes inject the coastal landscape with awe-inspiring drama.

A visitor *will* admire such scenic lyricism. Don't be alarmed if you see a line of cars

stopped by a roadside. Their passengers are merely taking time off to stop and stare. After all, there's nothing else they can do in a traffic jam on a country road. Conversely, when a train stops in the middle of a rice field, it is not necessarily waiting for passengers; more likely, a buffalo is loitering in its track and driver and passengers are staring, waiting for it to get out of the way.

"Slowly but surely", they say here. Time is not money. Time is not even time. In the main streets, in railway stations even, clocks tick their own time.

From the air, Gatotkaca's all encompassing vision sees the ruins of civilizations long buried in the soil and jungle tangle of Java. Foundations of temples and palaces, terracotta irrigation systems, and classical places such as Borobudur, Prambanan and Panataran still stand as awe-inspiring proofs of bygone eras.

Here too are remains of man's earliest ancestors — the Java Man. Fossils of this pre-historic man were unearthed in Central Java in 1890 and identified as the missing link in Darwin's theory of evolution. Eugene Dubois, a Dutch military physician, published information about his findings in 1894 and sparked off one of history's most fiercely debated controversies. The issue raged in academic circles for over two decades.

Today, appropriately perhaps, Java is the most densely populated part of Indonesia. With over 700 Java men (and women) to be found in every square kilometer of land, one has to be careful not to drop anything when flying. No matter where it lands, it is sure to hit someone on the head.

Even so, Java's people, geological riches and endearing beauty are celebrated by all acquainted with it. The island was recommended to visitors in an 1897 account of a Miss Scidmore's travels — *Java, the Garden of the East* — but no accolade can be more apt than that of Naturalist, Alfred R Wallace's. He pronounced Java a "noble and fertile island" and, echoing Miss Scidmore, "the very garden of the East."

Left: Indonesians call their nation "Our Land and Water". Three-fifths of Indonesia is sea, and the distinction between these primal elements is blurred. Water floods the land during harvest and monsoon and tons of topsoil enter the sea daily. Long stretches of Indonesian coastline, as near the village of Kalianak in East Java, are mangrove wetlands, an indeterminant region, neither wholly land nor sea, that plays an important role in the archipelago's ecology.

Javanese regard their island in no less romantic ways, often relating to it as they wish it to be and not as it is. For instance, the refrains of *Rayuan Pulau Kelapa*, a popular Javanese folk song, persist in singing praises of Java as a coconut isle when most of the island's beaches are empty of coconuts. One story goes so far as to claim Adam and Eve as Javanese, for though they were naked and had only an apple and a snake between them, they believed they were living in Paradise.

Javanese are a varied and colorful people. The Badui, for example, are direct descendants of the Pajajaran Empire and still preserve a millenium-old way of life in the isolated highlands of West Java where they have nothing to do with airplanes, automobiles, taxes and coins. Barter supplies all their needs. There is another unique point about Badui society. Though they live less than 160 kilometers from downtown Jakarta, they never lock their houses. There is nothing to steal.

Just 150 kilometers southeast of this timeless region, the city of Bandung stands head-over-heels in modernity. It must have been, once, the fastest growing city on earth. Hundreds of thousands of rural families rushed into its fold in the 1970s, snapping up the jobs created by new textile mills and other light, low-skill industries then beginning to mushroom. Now, with population densities of up to 90,000 per square meter, Bandung — once called the "Paris of Java" because of the wide and floral boulevards in its Dutch section — is fast becoming an urban nightmare. Resting on an ancient lake bed and encircled by mountains, the city is often invisible and enveloped in a murky fog. Perhaps these are the spirits of vanished waters, attempting, desperately, to drown the follies of man.

Spirits notwithstanding, rural folk continue their move into towns. They have little choice. Traditionally, each son is entitled to a fair share of a family's land. As the share shrinks with each new generation, some plots are now too small to support even a single person. The owner, lack-

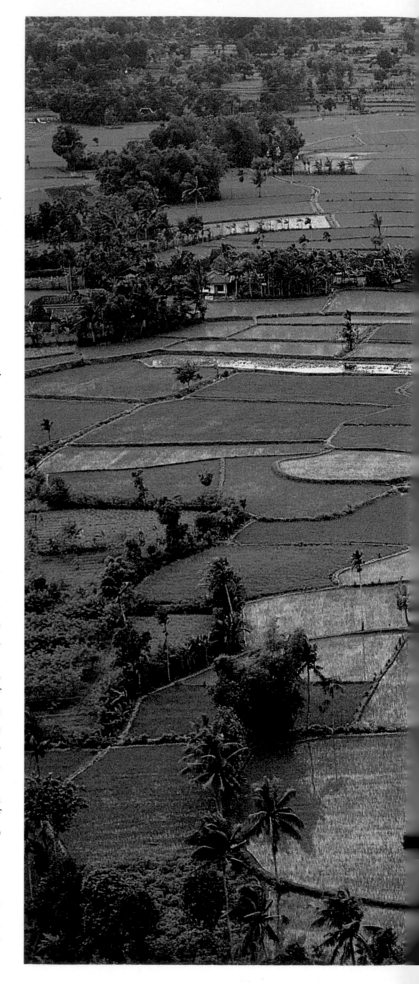

34

ing education and modern skills, sells out to become one of a growing army of landless.

The Government has one answer to this problem: transmigration. In a swift, clean break from old lives, entire families fly off to new homes carved out of the forests of Sumatra, Kalimantan or Irian Jaya. Trading a one quarter hectare of Javanese land for a two hectare plot and a bonus of a year's supply of rice and a concrete house, these transmigrants battle floods, drought and other social obstacles to build a new life on their nation's frontier.

Those who remain in Java are not forgotten. New infrastructures abound. Canals diverted to the southern sea direct floodwaters away from Yogyakarta and Solo. Sometimes, however, monsoon waters from the countrysides still surge down these canals and flood the cities. New roads cut across ricefields and through villages, or through land used for livelihood. These roads are quiet, with few large vehicles, and well illustrate a proverb that warns people to "Open your umbrella before the rain".

New or old, roads are where all Java comes together. From the air, you will see every type of Javanese locomotion ambling along the same narrow, potholed blacktop. Giant diesel trucks and buses, shiny, grand Mercedes and BMWs, screeching Japanese motorcycles, man-pedaled *becaks* — all must take their places behind the plodding ox cart.

Javanese roads seldom go directly from one place to another. They meander through the lush ricefields, turning left and right for no apparent reason, looping through the hinterland, branching into sidepaths, but ultimately delivering you to your destination — just like a Javanese conversation.

BALI FROM THE AIR. An author once wrote that this island belonged to the gods, the spirits of the earth and the nymphs. Small wonder. The land itself is art. Rice terraces add a flowing beauty to volcanic mountainsides, temples seemingly grow from oceanside cliffs, and dazzling white sand beaches outline an emerald isle set in an aquamarine sea. Bali, the so-called

Left: Paying the Bills. A Pertamina tanker takes on oil at the Cilacap refinery in West Java. Oil and gas exports account for the bulk of Indonesia's foreign earnings. But the heady oil boom years are over, and Indonesia must develop other export commodities.

Right: Indonesians often regard their ancestors as 'Champions of the Sea', but never as 'Champions' of the rivers that are equally important in daily life. However, rivers in Java have largely been supplanted by new, extensive highways.

"Morning of the World" and "Magic Isle", still breathes life into hackneyed tourist cliches.

From the air, you will see the genius of Bali, the reconciliation of native and foreign, old and new. Temple complexes stand beside first-class hotels, both with stone statues clothed in the checkered *sarung* of a deity standing guard at their gates. A trance dancer by night is a stone mason by day, carrying a sack of cement instead of a flower offering on his head. A beach is crowded with half-naked Europeans while, behind a clump of trees, a somnolent cow grazes. A procession of women with offerings on their heads and men playing a portable gamelan parades past hotels, restaurants and discos. Buses disgorge hundreds of tourists into a theatre to watch "authentic Balinese dancing," while next door, behind the walls of a family temple, a *Topeng* dancer becomes a god as he dons a power-laden mask to re-enact mythic tales in dance.

Bali is still a bit of heaven on earth. No visitor remains umoved by his stay on this "Island of the Gods", and most vow to return. Those who dream of living in Bali forever, though, must remember that, while anyone can visit, no one (except Balinese perhaps), can actually live in Paradise forever.

The farflung islands of the east and the north east makes up two-thirds of the Indonesian archipelago. And they are best seen from the air — their roads being few and in bad repair. Even their former colonial names are bywords for the ends of the earth: West Irian, Borneo, the Moluccas — the rich and fabulous Spice Islands.

Throughout NUSA TENGGARA, the islands east of Bali, small boats are the principal means of transport. From these small boats the people can truly experience the immensity of nature — the great sea. They fish alone, like old men of the sea. Or, like the crew of the *Pequod*, they set out in their tiny boats, hand-thrown spears ready, in search of migrating whales.

A rough people for a rough life. In Flores, it is said, teenagers have two life choices: fish, or enter the seminary. From the air, you will see

37

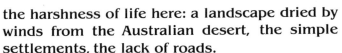

the harshness of life here: a landscape dried by winds from the Australian desert, the simple settlements, the lack of roads.

SULAWESI is to the east. From the air, the coast south of Ujung Pandang looks little different from the days of a visiting Joseph Conrad. On the beaches are the skeletons of half-completed Bugis *prahus* — 100-ton wooden ships constructed with simple tools; offshore, *prahus* sail with cargoes of copra and timber, as in past centuries.

KALIMANTAN FROM THE AIR. This is Indonesian Borneo — where the jungle rules. In the jungle, Dayaks hunt with ancient blowpipes the birds and monkeys which cohabit their realm. From the air, the red of Kalimantan's infertile clay earth in logged or burnt out areas is visible. Canopies of centuries old trees shield the jungle floor from sun and rain, but once men remove these trees, the few centimeters of fertile topsoil are quickly washed away.

IRIAN JAYA, the last frontier, is a sleeping giant clothed in snow-capped peaks and untouched valleys. From the air, you will see mud and thatch *honnays* of Baliem Valley tribesmen nestling in groves, while nearby the concrete houses of missionaries and development workers stand exposed to the full force of mountain winds. In open air markets, Javanese administrators in khaki safari suits walk among male Danis who wear only a *koteka* — a penis sheath — on bodies covered in cold-warding pig fat.

THE MOLUCCAS, where money once grew on trees, and men, heady with expectations, fought for supremacy. Every man, woman or child has , at one time or another, been acquainted with the fabled Spice Islands: the enchanted source of cloves, nutmegs, pepper, cinnamon and mace. It's not for nothing the Indonesians call it Maluku — the land of the King. But, despite its illustrious part in history, the Moluccas is today the most remote and least visited of Indonesia's provinces. From the air, the 999 islands are as jewels upon an enchanted ocean. *Bhinneka Tunggal Ike:* Unity in Diversity. This is Indonesia as seen from the air.

Left: A miniature world in a larger-than-life city, Jakarta's Dunia Fantasi (Fantasy Land) provides a quick world-tour for Indonesians unable to travel overseas. This Disneyland-like theme park is the first of its type in Southeast Asia. The exhibits are controlled by the latest Western technology, but the animated dolls are produced by old craftsmen in hundreds of small traditional shops.

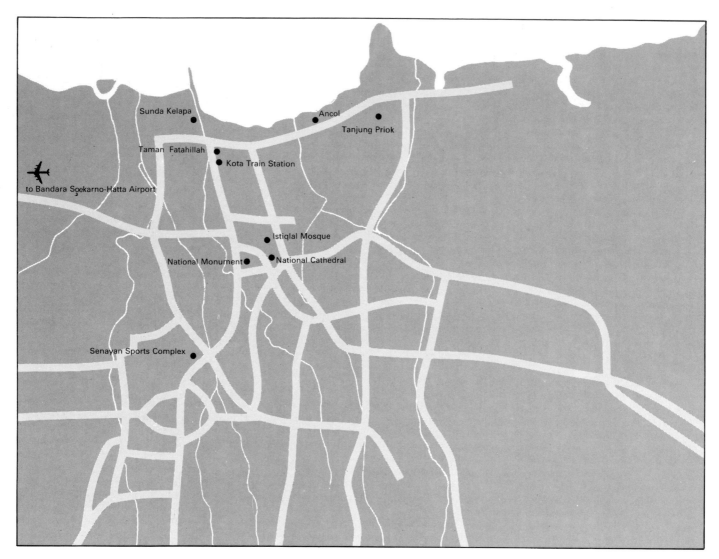

Sunda Kelapa

Ancol

Tanjung Priok

Taman Fatahillah

Kota Train Station

to Bandara Soekarno-Hatta Airport

Istiqlal Mosque

National Monument • National Cathedral

Senayan Sports Complex

This capital city of central Java — with its population of seven million — is a melting pot of diverse races, creeds and cultures, a fascinating mix of past and future Indonesia, the epitome of this growing and developing country. Total land area is 560 square kilometers. Its international airport, Bandara Soekarno-Hatta Airport, lies 23 kilometers west of the city's center.

Preceding Pages: The Pertamina refinery at Balikpapan casts an eerie glow on the warm Makassar Strait. During colonial times, Menteng was the genteel southern fringe of the city. Now it sits in Jakarta's geographic centre, its century-old mansions housing embassies and corporate managers.

jacatra nommee depuis Batavia

THE CAPITAL CITY

JAKARTA FROM THE AIR. Indonesia's capital city confronts the winged visitor with no apologies, licensed as it were, to disrupt the blue-green lyricism of the rest of surrounding Java with its own neon signs and mirrored facades. Here in this one city is all Indonesia has to offer. Every facet of the Indonesian experience — its people, its food, its culture — is represented within this 560 square kilometer tight city, to be slowly but surely uncovered and savored by the intrepid visitor.

Jakarta is a linear city, a fact best appreciated from the air. Lines of gleaming highrises and expressways snake their way through pockets of villages. The city seems alive — organic, at least. Old shophouses with peeling walls sag visibly in the oppressive midday heat. An inexorable tide of clapboard shacks overflows overnight onto vacant land. A great mass of urban housing and related paraphernalia hug the recently decommissioned Kemayoran airport, like a hungry amoeba ready to devour its prey.

Here, heterogeneity is taken to spectacular lengths. The white marble dome of the Istiqlal Mosque, Southeast Asia's largest, stands close to the wrought-iron steeples of the neo-Gothic National Cathedral: a bird can glide from one to the other with one strong flap of its wings. One neighborhood can contain a mix of Javanese, Sumatrans, Bugis, Irianese, Chinese, Indians, and a European or two.

All have come to Jakarta searching for a better life, for the capital is Indonesia's pot of gold at the end of a multi-ethnic rainbow. The amount of money circulating in this city alone is much greater than the sum-total in the rest of Indonesia. This money is not found only in the highrises or century-old mansions in Menteng or brand-new Spanish colonial villas in Pondok Indah. Here, even a tiny, cluttered hardware store in Chinatown might turn over US$100,000 a month. In some neighborhoods, homes of the superstitious, newly-rich expand with alacrity into adjoining lots.

Jakarta is perennially on the list of the ten most expensive cities in the world. Yet thousands of families live here on US100 dollars a month — or less. *"Who Sent You To Jakarta?"*, asks a folksong from Manado. The answer, always, is: *"I came of my own choice."*

The city is home to seven million people described variously as funny, fun-loving, irreverent and irrepressible. Even so, the projected growth rate of over 300 per cent by the year 2005 is alarming. Already in some parts of town, the population density is a crammed 40,000 per square kilometer. By the year 2000, there will be 23.5 million Jakartans. The land too will be expanded on with the hope of accommodating the growing multitude. Neighboring towns have begun to give way to a new identity. Bekasi, Bogor and Tangerang will soon be Jabotabek, a new name on the map.

For the moment, Jakarta remains a city of endless choice. You can travel around in anything from a limousine to a pedicab, sleep in a five star hotel or a five dollar a night dormitory. If you accept Jakarta on its own terms, it will give you anything you want. If you fight it, as will the uninitiated visitor in a hurry, Jakarta will strike back five-fold.

During the monsoon, however, Jakarta fights back whether or not you keep your side of the bargain. Neighborhoods are turned into lakes and roads to rivers in the blink of an eye. Buses ploughing through the flooded streets drench hapless pedestrians and motorcyclists mercilessly. The city's street urchins live for the rainy season, learning early to thrive in adversity. When your car stalls they are there to help push it along. When you are unprepared for rain, they are waiting at the bus-stops: umbrellas in their hands, anticipation in their eyes. They also learn to profit from inconvenience.

Jakartans have been trying for centuries to overcome the flooding. During the 5th century AD, Purnawarman of the Taruma Negara kingdom dug a canal to direct water to the sea, finishing 6,122 dams along the canal's 11 kilometer length in barely 21 days. The king

Left: Jakarta is a linear city, a collection of villages with a modern city winding through them like a steel and glass river. This melange of soaring skyscrapers, mansions, kitschy monuments, and endless tracts of mean shops and houses is the essence of Indonesia.

gave the Brahman priests 1,000 cattle in tribute. These days, those sacred cows sell quickly as *sate*, along with any other animal. Anything you want you can eat in Jakarta: green mussels, dog meat, and parts of other animals.

From the air, you will see restaurant signs strung along the entire length of nearly any road: giant, garish neon billboards advertising cavernous Chinese eating palaces that look like used car lots; faded, flickering signs touting traditional fried chicken restaurants whose old Javanese recipe is the only advertisement they need; and, here and there, the floodlit goatee of the ubiquitous Kentucky Colonel.

To eat like a Jakartan, however, you must hit the streets. From the air, the canvas-roofs of *warungs* look like endless rows of Bedouin encampments on the streets. In their shelter are people tucking into delicious, aromatic *sate* — grilled goat or chicken meat on a skewer — or fried rice, noodles and grilled fish. Most *warungs*, like Bedouins, fold up their tents and steal away by dawn, but enough remain on the roadside to seriously impede traffic in the day. They are often joined by street sellers, and if that were not enough, workers continually tear up and fill in the pavement.

Jakarta's horrendous traffic jams are graphic delights from the air. The metal tops of brightly colored Toyotas (popular made-in-Japan cars) line the streets from end to end as one long, ill arranged jigsaw glinting in the sun-light. But the traffic does move, only slowly. To tell the truth, traffic is seldom halted for more than a few minutes. Just when you vow to leave Jakarta for good, the road ahead opens, clear and fast, mocking you for your lack of faith.

So why hurry? In Jakarta, if a clerk hurries to his job, his friends ask: *"Why such a rush? The office will still be there tomorrow."*

The office will certainly be there, but it will not be the same. A melting pot on a furious boil, Jakarta is rapidly changing, adapting, accommodating, occasionally spilling over. Jakarta is becoming a newly adolescent city with four centuries of history behind her.

Left: Indonesia's principal port, Tanjung Priok harbor, was established in 1887. Today this modern harbor handles most of the country's vast domestic and international shipping.

Below: Clutter at the base of Indonesia's symbol of independence as the Monas undergoes one of its periodic refurbishment. This last monument erected by former President Soekarno is a Hindu-Javanese lingga, *representing the power of the Indonesian people.*
Right: Istiqlal, the largest mosque in Southeast Asia. Jakarta has hundreds more; in many neighborhoods one on every corner.

Right: Though the prestigious banks and international corporations conduct business in the string of new office towers along Jalan Thamrin and Jalan Sudirman, Jalan Hayam Wuruk is Jakarta's economic powerhouse. Most of Jakarta's — and Indonesia's — money circulates around the cluttered offices and unprepossessing shops in Kota and Glodok.

Below: Erected 20 years ago on the fringes of Jakarta, the Welcome Monument now stands close to the city center. On the lower right stand the Hotel Indonesia, Indonesia's first international hotel. Once the pride of Jakarta, Hotel Indonesia is now struggling to hold its own against a dozen newer establishments.

Below: As Indonesia gains importance in world commerce, Jakarta has become a popular venue for conventions and trade fairs, many being held in the Jakarta Convention Hall in Senayan.
Right: The DPR, or House of Representatives, convenes in this building.

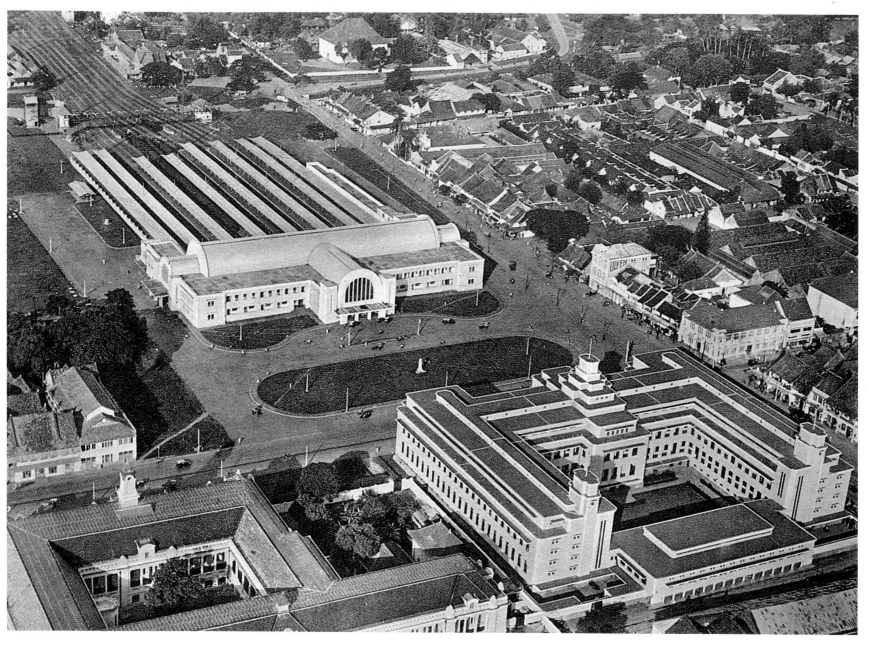

Right: Jakartans constantly travel around the city and most times of day the buses are packed, though the conductor can always squeeze in one more passenger.
Far Right: Jin-de Yuan is Jakarta's oldest Chinese temple. A large population of ethnic Chinese have lived and worked in Jakarta since the early nineteenth century, largely retaining their own customs. These days, many Chinese are being assimilated into mainstream Indonesia.

Right: Senayan Sports Complex, built with Russian money in 1962, is Jakarta's premier sports venue. Up to 120,000 people can squeeze into the stadium for a football final, with the spectators' private cars and city buses halting traffic for hours.
Far Right: Keong Emas — the golden Snail — an IMAX system wide screen theatre showing the film 'Beautiful Indonesia' daily to tourists and locals.

Below and Right: The recreational complex at Ancol in North Jakarta sits on 187 hectares of reclaimed swamp. With an oceanarium, art market, swimming pools, sailing, Bina Ria Beach and the recently-completed Dunia Fantasi, Ancol is an all-round amusement center.

Below and Right: "Little boxes, little boxes ...." Many middle class Jakartans are forsaking the chaotic jumble of the inner city for new housing developments in the suburbs.

Below: The town square, before the focus of Jakarta moved south, Fatahillah Square was renovated and converted into a tourist attraction during the 1970s. The three surrounding colonial edifices have become museums.

Below: "Little Holland in the Tropics" is an accurate description of Batavia – Colonial Jakarta. Homesick Dutchmen dug canals and lined them with European style buildings, many of which still stand in Kota and Sunda Kelapa. Right: 'Who Sent You To Jakarta', a folksong from Manado has become the theme song of the newcomers. The answer is 'I came of my own choice.'

SUMATRA

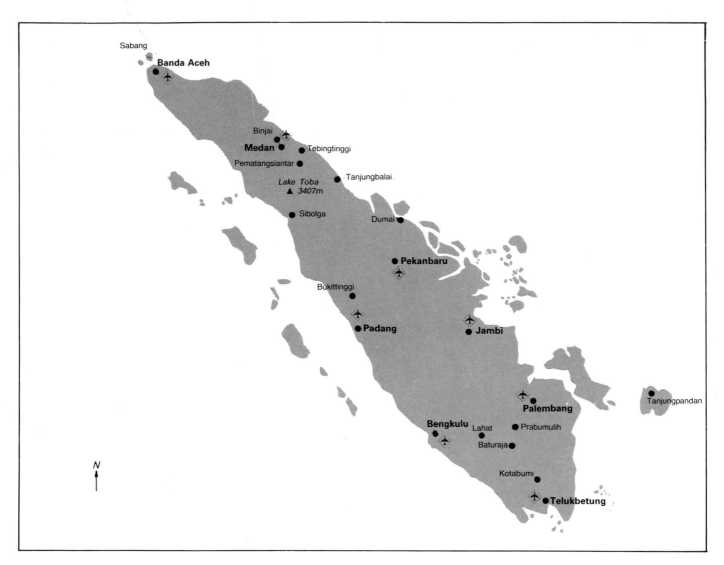

Its old name, *suma terra* (black earth), can still be found on old navigational maps. This refers to the dark and very fertile volcanic soil in the region. This second largest of the Sunda Islands measures 370,000 square kilometers and has a population of 32 million. Its dense rainforest is home to exotic fauna, countless types of apes, wild elephants, tigers, the rare Sumatram rhinoceros and friendly tribal people — the Bataks and Minangkabaus. Medan is the capital of the province of north Sumatra, Palembang that of South Sumatra and Padang of West Sumatra, all with airport facilities. Other large towns include Banda Aceh Pekanbaru, Jambi and Bengkulu. Highest elevation: the Kerinci (3,805m).

Preceding Pages: Operation Ganesha. Jeeps and helicopters were used to chase wild elephants out of Sumatra's croplands. Right: Lake Toba, the largest lake in Southeast Asia, home of the Bataks and popular tourist resort.

Plantation crops: Oil Palm (below) and Tea (right) have long been key crops in North Sumatra. In some areas, new plantations have outstripped processing capacity. For want of a factory, some oil palm fruit is sold as firewood.

Left: Maimoon Palace, Medan. Built in 1888 for the Sultan of Deli, Maimoon Palace typifies coastal Malay architecture. Malay cultural influence is still strong in eastern Sumatra, as mainland Malaysia in just a short hop across the Malacca Strait, while Java is two days' sail south.

Far left: Though the Batak are primarily Christian, Islam is strong in cosmopolitan Medan. Like Singapore, Medan is a mix of Asian cultures.

Right: Much of Sumatra's plantation and mineral wealth is shipped through Belawan harbor near Medan. Sumatra is Indonesia's economic back bone, producng oil, forest products, rubber, palm oil, tea, and other money spinning commodities.

Below: The special industrial zone at Batam, 20 kilometers south of Singapore. This strategic island – jungle and mudflats ten years ago – is being developed into an industrial, shipping and tourist center.

Right: Taming Sumatra's Ashahan River. Draining giant Lake Toba, the Ashahan is harnessed to provide power for rapidly industrializing North Sumatra. Far right: Switching station for Ashahan Dam.

Far Right: The Alas River tumbles from its source on Gunung Lueser in North Sumatra. For the first 100 kilometers, the Alas flows through Mount Lueser National Park, an important wildlife reserve. Right: Once out of the park, the Alas becomes leaden with mud from logged-off mountains and meanders through the lowlands toward the Indian Ocean.

JAVA

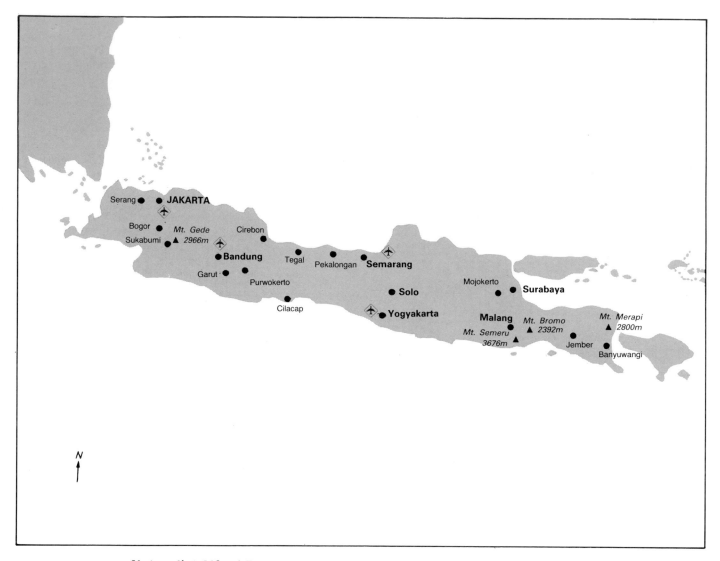

Naturalist Alfred Russell Wallace described Java as "that noble and fertile island — the very Garden of the East". About 100 million people live on some 132,187 square kilometers of land. Two-thirds of these, however, are packed into only seven per cent of the total land area, making its population density twice that of the central European states. Rice, tea, tobacco and coffee plantations form a large part of the lush and scenic Javanese countryside. Its capital city Jakarta has a population of seven million. Its international airport, Bandara Soekarno-Hatta Airport, lies 23 kilometers to the west. Highest elevation: Semeru (Mahameru) 3,676m. Other major cities include Yogyakarta, Surakarta (Solo), Surabaya, Bandung (City of Flowers) and Semarang — all of which, except for Surakarta, have their own airport facilities.

Preceding Pages: "... as though the gods had created a masterpiece using the earth as a canvas. This is not Art for Arts's sake, as these beautiful fields have changed us from a rice importing to a food self-sufficient nation."
Right: Classic Central Java. A stately river flows through an intricate mosaic of lush, green paddies. The same scenery that enchanted nineteenth century travellers like Miss Scidmore is little changed.

Right: Subtle shadings of the Java Sea create this piece of minimalistic art. Far Right: Only 40 kilometers from Jakarta, the Thousand Islands

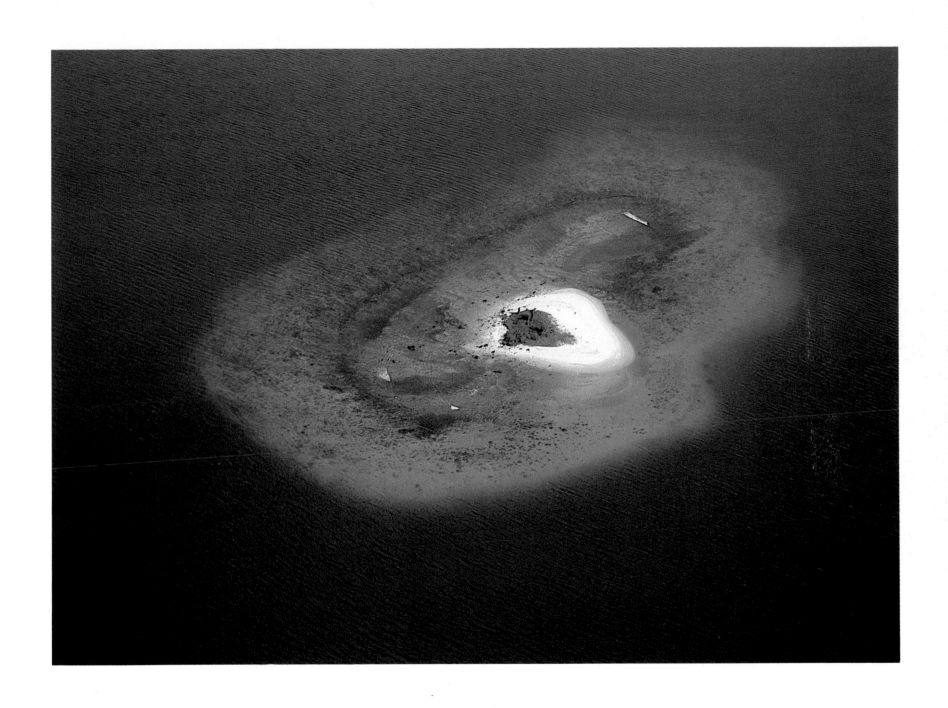

Below and Right: A flour mill and sawmill near Tanjung Priok attest to Indonesia's downstream production capacity. Once hewers of wood and drawers of water – or oil in this case – Indonesia is sending increasing amounts of refined goods overseas.

Jakarta's escape valves. The mountains south of Jakarta have long provided a refreshing break for Jakarta's sweltering residents. Below: Bogor Palace was the weekend retreat of Dutch governors and later, President Soekarno.

*Left: These days,
Jakartans go beyond
Bogor to the hotels,
swimming pools and
tennis courts of the
Puncak resort.*

*Below: Karawang on the north coast is called the "rice barn of Java".
Flat and uninteresting, Java's north coast is Indonesia's most
important agricultural and industrial area. But, rice is losing its
traditional priority to encroaching industrial estates.*

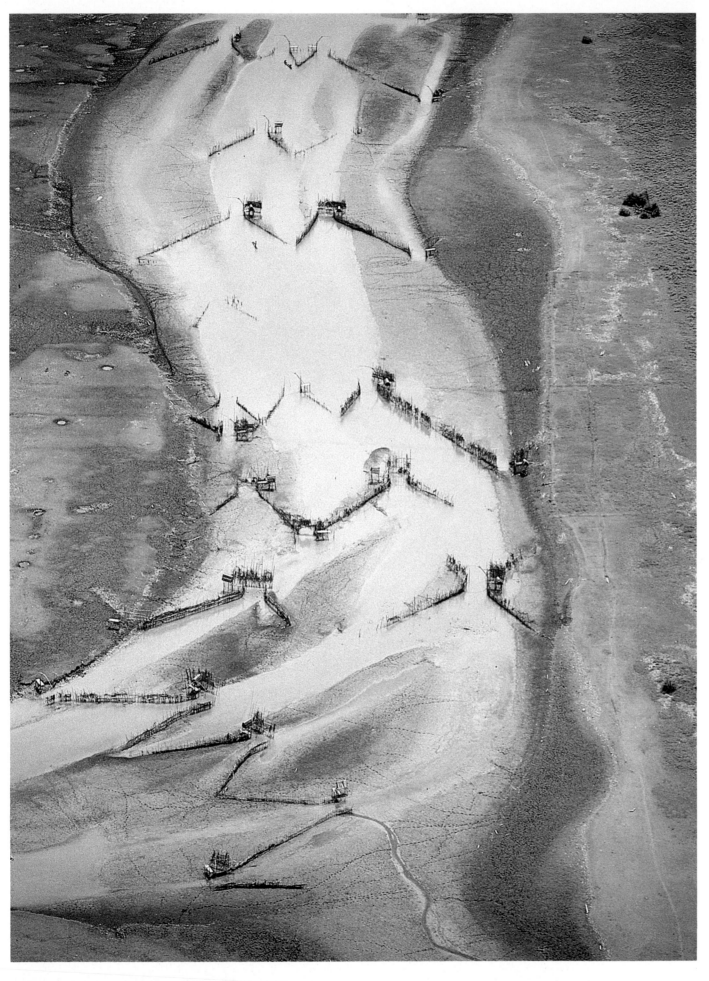

Far left: Mount Galungung blows its top. Emperiling airliners at 30,000 feet, dust clouds from a long series of eruptions in 1982 wreaked havoc over most of West Java.
Left: Palm leaves sag under the weight of dust and ashes that blanket the villages around Galunggung, forcing thousands to flee.
Left, Below: A green banana leaf promises life will return to desolation. Given time, the dust and ash recharge the soil with incredible fertility.

*Below: Ambarawa, a security "fortress" near Majelang Central Java,
built by Dutch colonialists.*

Below: A herringbone pattern of fishing crafts line the Losari River near Cirebon in West Java.

Jatiluhur, West Java: Hi-Tech and Harnessing Nature. Below: Palapa communications sateliites ground station at Jatiluhur. Indonesia is relying heavily on satellite to tie the far-flung islands of the archipelago.

Left: Jatiluhur Dam on the Citarum River, Indonesia's first hydropower project. The power of Citarum is also being tapped at Saguling and Cirata to feed West Java's insatiable demand for electricity.

Below and Right: The Dutch said the East Indies 'gird the equator like a string of emeralds'. The islands of Indonesia inspire such vexing lyricism in all but the most jaded writers.

Left: Recreating the glory of lost empires to improve the balance of payments, the millenium-old Hindu Prambanan temple complex near Yogyakarta is being restored as part of Indonesia's drive to attract more tourists. Below: Candi Kalasan near Prambanan, built in 778 AD, is the oldest Mahayana Buddhist temple in Java.

115

116

Left: A city within a city, the Yogyakarta Kraton is still a functioning palace. The seventeenth century styles and customs live on, only grudgingly acknowledging the modern world outside. Far left: Indonesia's historic Garuda Hotel has been completely renovated. The refurbished suites in the two original wings retain the ambience of stately, graceful, colonial Java.

Right: Susunan Palace in Solò, severely damaged by fire in 1985, is being restored to former glory. Foremen and workers wear ceremonial sashes and headscarves on site to placate palace spirits who might otherwise be offended by their coarse manners. Below: Mangkunegaran Palace, home of Solo's junior royal family, is open to the public. In fact, part of the compound has been converted into a hotel.

Below: Buffaloes are still the most efficient in ploughing the tiny, muddy ricefields of Central Java, such as these near Kediri.

Left: Indonesian potato chips, krupuk are the classic Indonesian snack. These wafer-thin rice cakes are dried in the sun, hand-packed in plastic bags and shipped to warungs throughout Java. Fried, they balloon into airy crackers that go well with rice, soup, or cold beer.

Right: The subtle understatement of an ornamental pool at the Gudang Garam Kretek cigarette factory in Kediri. Far Right: "Like smoking desert ...." is one description of kretek clove cigarettes. After decades of wide-spread popularity in Indonesia, factories like Gudang Garam now exports large quantities.

123

Javanese cities are noisy and bustling, but most towns which functioned as colonial administrative centers, like Lawang (left) and **Malang,** *have quiet, refreshing town squares. Much colonial architecture remains in Indonesia, though the solid houses and art-deco office blocks of the Dutch era are being demolished to make way for American style shopping centers.*

Left: Of the legacies left by the Dutch, one of the most appreciated is Indonesia's version of Heineken Pilsener. The Bintang Brewery in Surabaya produces Indonesia's favorite beer.
Far left: A church in Surabaya. Christianity has come to East Java, though the area is still overwhelmingly muslim.

Below: Ferry-terminal for crossing from Surabaya to Madura; a half-hour crossing. Right: Dutch godowns and Bugis prahus line the Kalimas canal in Surabaya. Once the East Indies' greatest trading city, Surabaya has now become a less exuberant industrial center.

Below: Low-cost tract housing for factory workers near Gresik. Many companies, institutions, and government agencies provide housing for their long-term employees.
Right: Once a quaint town of traditional woodworkers, Gresik has expanded into a major industrial area during the past ten years.

131

Right and Far Right: Life is easier for the fishermen living beside the shallow, gentle Java Sea, as in the village of Camplong in Madura, than it is for those who must brave the stormy Indian Ocean.

Below and Right: The dry north coast of Java's eastern salient has a mediterranean feel. Baluran Game Park on Java's northeastern tip is mainly savannah — a bit of Africa in the East Indies.

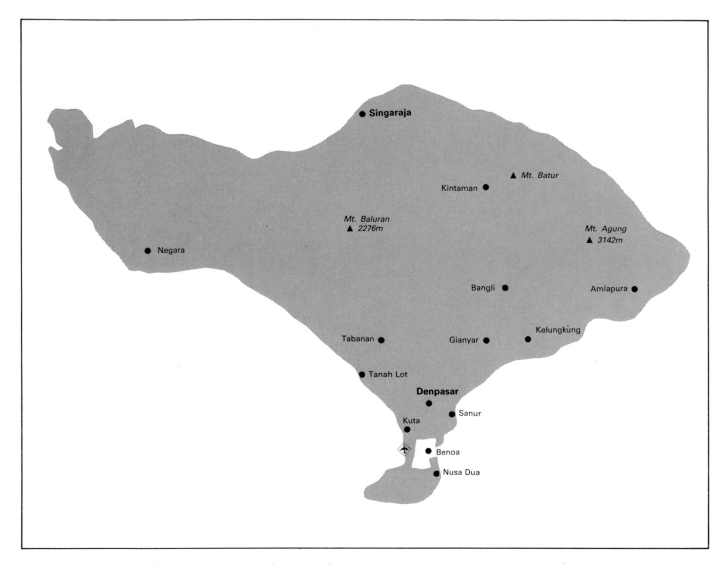

Map of Bali showing: Singaraja, Mt. Batur, Kintaman, Mt. Baluran ▲ 2276m, Mt. Agung ▲ 3142m, Negara, Bangli, Amlapura, Tabanan, Gianyar, Kelungkung, Tanah Lot, Denpasar, Sanur, Kuta, Benoa, Nusa Dua

Bali, *pulau dewata, island of the gods and demons,* has been given different names by different people. They say "this particular piece of earth belongs to the gods, the spirits of the earth and to the nymphs." About 2.8 million people live on this 5,600 square kilometer island. Bali's international airport, Ngurah Rai, lies five kilometers south of *Kuta* — an endless stretch of white sand and a surfer's dream. *Denpasar,* Bali's capital, is the largest city with 200,000 people. *Sanur* and *Nusa Dua* are other lively seaside resorts. Highest elevation: Gunung Agung (3,142m).

Preceding Pages: Temples line a hillside near Kintamani in the classic Bali panorama.

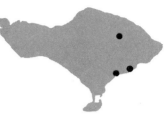

Left: In Kusamba, only a few kilometers from the bustle of the tourist spots, Balinese make salt by evaporating sea water.

Below: "In Bali, a complex irrigation method called subak ensures each farmer receives his proper share of water. You cannot see this directly, but you can sense it in the smiles of farmers ..." Right: Ricefields near Tirtaganga.

Below: Cruise ships began calling at Padangbai harbor in Bali during the 1930s, provoking fears among foreign residents that the scores of tourists would destroy local culture. As it turned out, neither the cruise passengers, package tourists, backpackers, nor even Hollywood's Love Boat made any negative impact on Balinese culture.

Left: Regular ferry services connect the major islands, such as this ship plying daily between Padangbai harbor, Bali and Mataram, Lombok. But many Indonesians still rely on traditional wooden boats to move between the remote islands of the archipelago.

Left: This opulent water palace at Karangasem, Amalapura, was a favorite retreat of King Anak Agung Angluah Ketut, the last and most cultured Balinese Raja. The lake and pavilions surrounding the king's bungalow represent the calm waters of the Hindu cosmos. Below: A typical Balinese family compound with different houses for sleeping, eating, praying, and other domestic activities.

Far Right: 'Bali Hai Living.' The walled-in tourist enclave at Nusa Dua. For all the concern about the impact of tourism on Balinese society, the regular tourist seldom strays from the luxurious laps of Sanur, Nusa Dua, and Kuta. In upcountry Bali, life goes on pretty much as before. Top left: Bali Sol Hotel in Nusa Dua. Below: Bali Beach Hotel, in Sanur.

151

Below and Right: A rugged version of Bali, Lombok is an intriguing mixture of Balinese and Malay muslim influence – multi-tiered Hindu temples and gleaming white mosques overlook the same ricefields. Lombok even has its own Kuta Beach, a deserted stretch of sand where Lombok youths gather each year on February 2 to sing pantuns *– Malay poems – in a traditional courtship ritual.*

*Below: Waikelo Harbor in East Sumba where the land
is dry and rocky and inhospitable. But the ikat weavings
produced here are collectible items overseas.
Right: The western side of Komodo, the island in beween
Sumbawa and Flores. Only about 500 people live here making
a living from fishing. The land is mostly barren.*

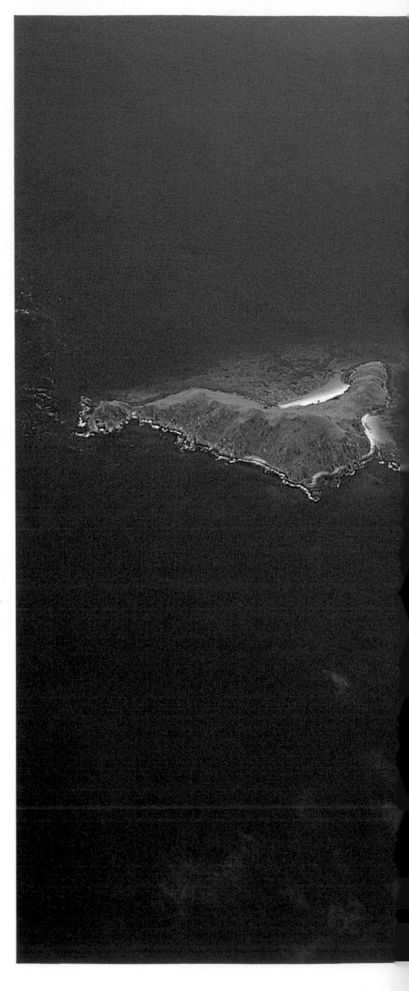

Left: Mount Amalomba in Flores. Sitting right on the Pacific Ocean's Ring of Fire, Indonesia experiences frequent major eruptions.

Far left: Any large structure on Flores is likely to be a church. St Francis Xavier charged through these islands in 1547, leaving thousands of Catholic converts in his wake. Today, East Nusa Tenggara is 80 percent Christian.

Right: "Just when you are utterly fed up with the noise, heat, crowds, hassles, rip-offs, and the hundreds of petty annoyances of tropical life, you pass the beach during sunset and fall in love with the place all over again." – an Old Indonesia Hand.
Below: Sails golden in the setting sun, the twin masted catamarans of Florenese fishermen cruise the Sawu Sea.

Below: Slash and burn agriculture in Kalimantan. A section of forest is cut, burned off, then sown with rice or cassava. After two harvests, the land lies fallow for several years while the farmer repeats the process in another forest tract. Right: "... to enter the lonely stretches of sparkling water bordered by the dense and silent forest, whose big trees nodded their outspread boughs gently in the faint, warm breeze — as if in sign of tender but melancholy welcome."
Joseph Conrad — An Outcast of the Islands.

*Right and Far Right:
Convinced they will
become ill if their houses
do not stand in water, the
Bajau build their
communities on tidal flats
and shallow bays. The last
of Southeast Asia's
nomadic seafarers, Bajau
are settling in several
areas of East Indonesia.*

Right: Highway, fishpond, reservoir, sewer; life centers around the wide, lazy, tea-colored rivers of East Kalimantan. River settlements are typically a single line of houses — erected on stilts to cope with wet season flooding — stretching up to three kilometers along the river.

*Below: In Kalimantan, people travel the rivers daily — whole families
sitting in a hollowed log with scarcely five centimeters of freeboard.*

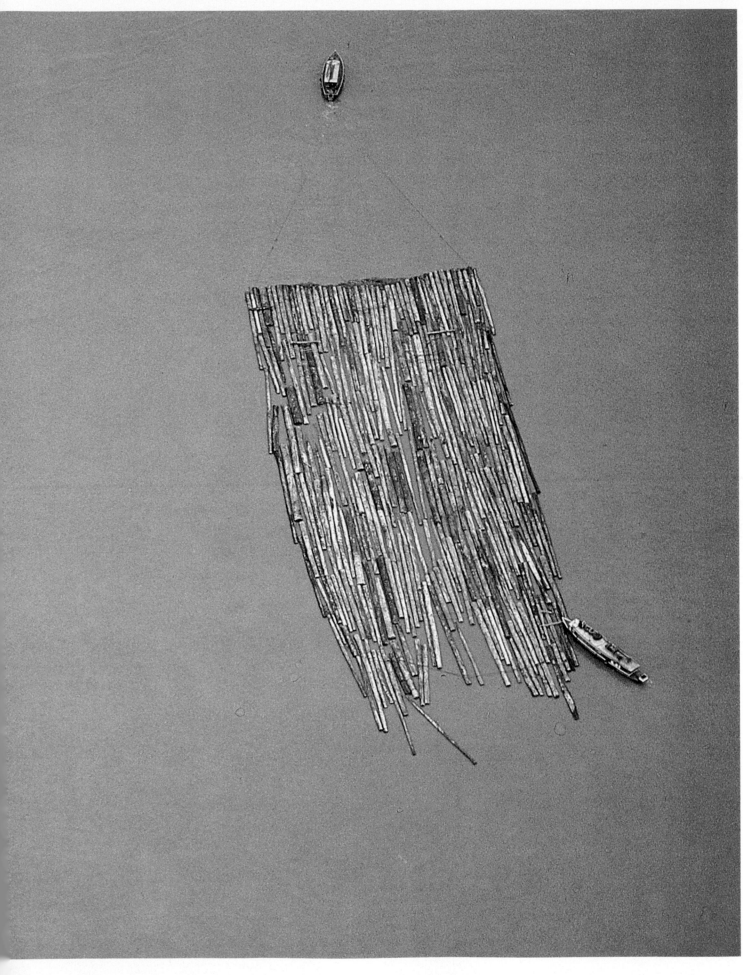

Left: "Disdainful kings of the Borneo jungle ...." now felled, boomed, and floated down the Mahakam river for export. Timber is an important export commodity, but large tracts of primary jungle are being destroyed by extensive logging and inadequate replanting.

SULAWESI

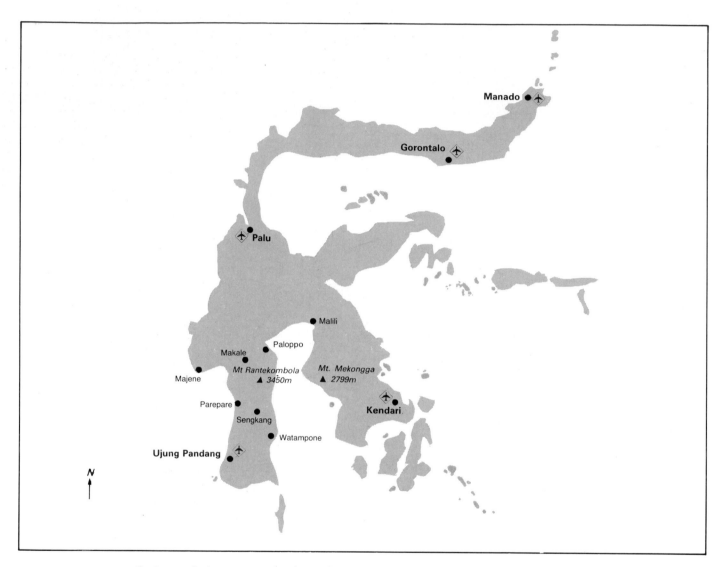

Sulawesi has something for everyone — hissing volcanoes, bubbling hot springs, sandy white beaches that go on forever, green and blue lakes, virgin rainforests teeming with the most fascinating wild life, friendly open people with a love for colorful celebrations, and world famous sea gardens. The island, which frequently appears as "Celebes" in atlases, resembles a beautiful orchid from the air. Total land area measures 189,000 square kilometers. There are about 11 million inhabitants. Sulawesi is divided into north, central, south and east Sulawesi. Capital cities are Manado, Palu, Ujung Pandang and Kendari. Airport: Hasunudin. Highest elevation: Rantekombola (3,450m).

*Preceding Pages: Though
the Bugis are renowned as
mariners, most Bugis
return to their villages to
farm after retiring from
the sea at age 35. As
arable land is scarce in
South Sulawesi, Bugis
have migrated to other
islands in the archipelago.
Sizable Bugis settlements
exist in Sumatra, Irian
Jaya, and Malaysia.
Left: Fried noodles, boiled
peanuts, and other late
afternoon snacks are sold
along the Pantai Losari
seawall in Ujung Pandang.
Unlike many Indonesian
cities, Ujung Pandang,
cooled by sea breezes and
steeped in history, is a
pleasant place to visit.
Formerly the major
colonial port of Makassar,
Ujung Pandang is still an
important shipping
center, the home base of a
thousand Bugis ships.*

Left: Fort Rotterdam, a 17th Century Dutch fortress, once safeguarded the important trading city of Makassar in South Sulawesi. Makassar is now called Ujung Pandang, and the fort is a museum.
Below: "The seagoing equivalent of the unlicenced taxis that clog Indonesian streets", Bugis sailing prahus maintain a precarious niche in the archipelago's shipping network.

Left: "From the air, we see a new river pushing through the jungle. A journey requiring a day by boat on the old rivers, takes an hour by bus on the new." Below: This village in Toraja is a two-day walk to the nearest road, but is not isolated. The narrow footpaths winding through the mountains are used by a steady stream of traders and the occasional intrepid Western tourist.

Right: The roofs of the traditional Tongkongan houses resemble the prows of the legendary ships that carried the Toraja people to Tanah Toraja, South Sulawesi. Like the Batak of Sumatra and the Dayak of Kalimantan, the Toraja are Proto-Malays, the first Indo-chinese people to settle the archipelago.

Below: The Toraja bury their dead in cliffside crypts that could take two years to chisel. Elaborate Toraja funeral ceremonies – which involve the ritual slaughter of scores of buffaloes and other animals to feed the hundreds of guests – reaffirm the complex system of privilege and obligation that holds Toraja society together.
Right: A village in Tanah Toraja.

IRIAN JAYA

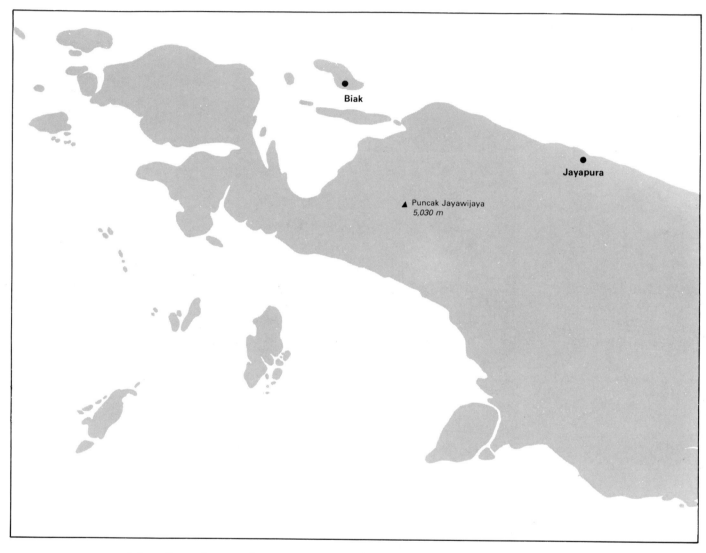

Irian Jaya forms the western portion of New Guinea, the world's second largest island. This land mass has been a province of the Republic of Indonesia since 1969. It occupies 420,000 square kilometers and has an estimated 1.3 million native inhabitants who call themselves Papuans. Few tourists have ventured into this unspoilt land and, for those who do, be advised that sign language is not exactly safe to use with the reserved and isolated cultures of Irian Jaya. A basic knowledge of Bahasa Indonesia, however, is useful. The cities of Jayapura, Timuka and Sorong, as well as the island of Biak, can be reached from Jakarta by Merpati Airlines and from Surabaya, Ujung Pandang and Ambon by Garuda Airways. A good pair of comfortable, medium weight hiking shoes with a heavy tread, mosquito repellant spray, extra socks and shoelaces would be appropriate for an expedition into this remote region.
Highest elevation: Puncak Jayawijaya (5,030m).

Below and right: Situated in one of the prettiest bays, Jayapura, the capital of Irian Jaya, is a large administrative center.

Right: For those unwilling to fly into the highlands, this is an alternative route. With the Trans-Irian Highway still years from completion, overland travel is next-to-impossible. Wamena, an important highland town, is two hours by air from Jayapura or a full month by land — if you survive. The rugged conditions attract a certain breed of people. When a young man in Wamena was asked who he was, he replied: "I am a pioneer." When asked what his job was, he said: "Well, pioneering."

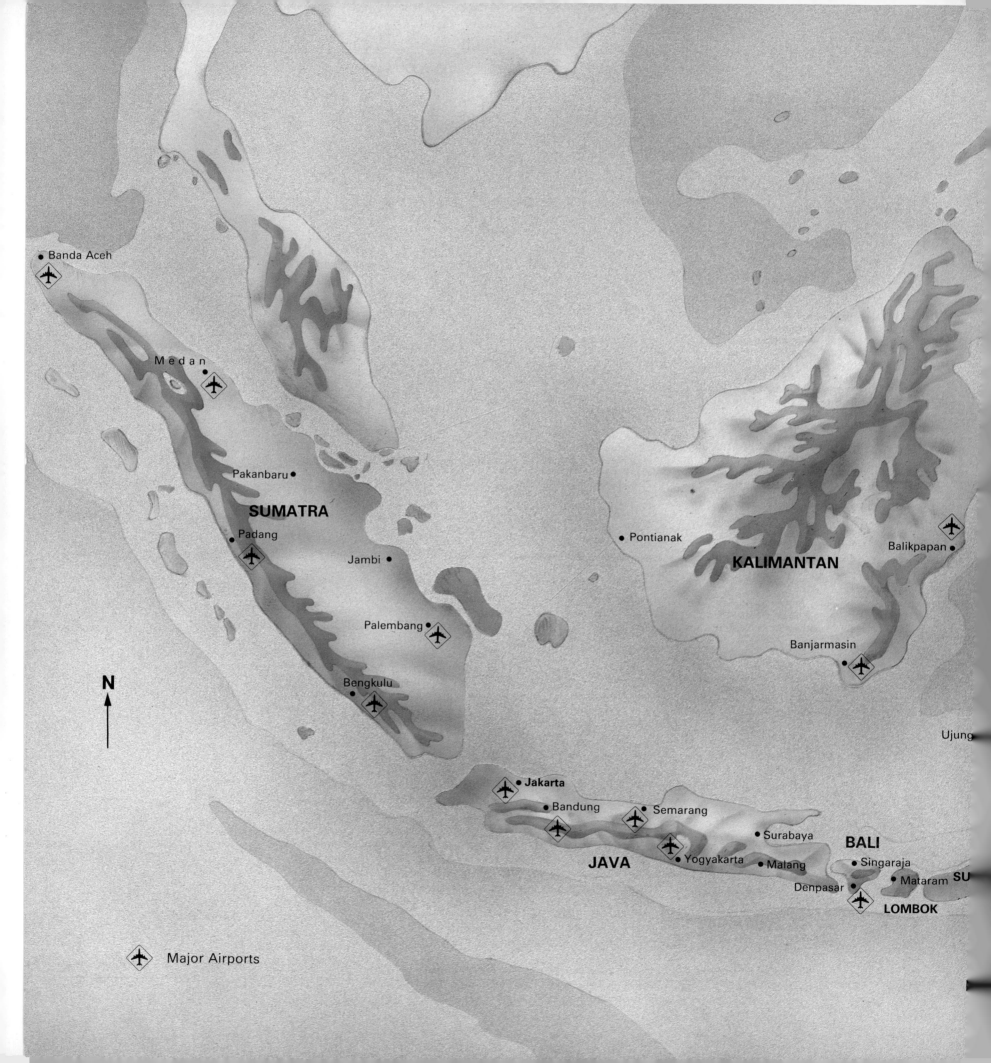

INDONESIA

The Indonesian archipelago comprises 13,677 islands and stretches 5,760 kilometers across the globe, making it the largest island state in the world. It straddles the equator, linking two continents — Asia and Australia — whilst separating the Indian Ocean and the Pacific Ocean. Climate is tropical with rainfall all year round and high mean temperature of 26 to 30 degrees centigrade. Indonesia has a total land area of two million square kilometers with 164 million inhabitants — making it the fourth most densely populated country in the world. Highest elevation: Puncak Jayawijaya (5,030m) in Irian Jaya.

• Manado

• Ternate

Gorontalo

HALMAHERA

• Palu

• Biak

SULAWESI

SERAM

BURU

Jayapura •

• Ambon

Kendari •

THE   MOLUCCAS

IRIAN JAYA

MODO

FLORES

• Dīli

JMBA

TIMOR

• Kupang

TENGGARA

INDEX